Published by
Joseph Rodriguez Trust
17151 University Ave
Sandy, Or 97055
United States

Cover and interior design by Joseph Rodriguez

Printed in the United States of America

First Edition

For more information, visit:
www.sandyjiujitsu.org

Guardian Mt. Hood Brazilian Jiu-Jitsu
Belt Curriculum & Student Handbook

by

Professor Joseph Rodriguez
Founder and Head Instructor
Guardian Mt. Hood Brazilian Jiu-Jitsu Academy

Welcome to Guardian Mt. Hood Brazilian Jiu Jitsu

From Professor Jose and Coach Angelica

Dear Students,

It is with deep respect and excitement that I welcome you to Guardian Mt. Hood. Here, you are not just stepping onto the mats to learn a martial art; you are stepping into a community, a shared path of growth, discipline, and wisdom. We are more than a school, more than a place of practice; we are a family bound by the principles of Brazilian Jiu Jitsu, a philosophy rooted in overcoming obstacles through intellectual leverage rather than brute force.

At Guardian Mt. Hood, we believe that the greatest power lies not in strength alone but in understanding. Brazilian Jiu Jitsu teaches us how to leverage technique, timing, and strategy to neutralize any physical disadvantage. It shows us that the mind is the most important weapon in any confrontation. Here, we focus on mastering ourselves first—our emotions, our impulses, our fears—before mastering our opponents. In this way, we internalize one of the deepest truths of this art: the best fighters never fight. They use their wisdom, calm, and understanding to avoid conflict, and only engage when absolutely necessary, with precision and control.

You may hear often that we practice BJJ with the mindset of "being a warrior in the garden, rather than a gardener in the war." This idea captures the essence of our philosophy: we cultivate peace, but we train for the storm. We live with calm minds and disciplined hearts, yet we are prepared for the unexpected challenges life throws our way. To be unprepared in times of peace is to be vulnerable in times of conflict. That's why we train—to be ready, not for violence, but for life's inevitable hardships, with courage, strength, and intelligence.

We also emphasize that here, you will learn to "embrace the suck." There will be discomfort, frustration, and moments where the journey seems steep. But in those moments, we teach you to control your emotions, which are the first step toward controlling your body, and in turn, controlling any external threat. Learning this control teaches us that true power comes not from dominating others, but from mastering ourselves. It's this self-mastery that makes us resilient in the face of adversity, on and off the mats.

Guardian Mt. Hood operates not as a traditional business, but as a nonprofit community, dedicated to empowering individuals and bringing people together. We are not driven by profit, but by the mission to enrich lives, to create a safe space where anyone—regardless of background, gender, age, or physical ability—can grow, learn, and thrive. When you train here, you are not just a student; you are a vital part of a supportive and inclusive community. Together, we will push each other to be our best, not just as martial artists but as human beings.

Know that while you are here, you are encouraged to ask questions, think critically, and embrace the philosophical roots of Brazilian Jiu Jitsu. Each time you step onto the mats, you are cultivating not just physical skill, but wisdom, patience, and humility. You are preparing yourself not just for battle, but for life—learning to solve problems calmly and peacefully, with an unshakeable foundation built on discipline and control.

I encourage you to see this journey as more than just learning techniques; it is a path to a deeper understanding of yourself, your emotions, and the world around you. You will find that as you strengthen your body, your mind will sharpen, and as you master the art of Jiu Jitsu, you will come to embody the peace and wisdom we seek to cultivate here.

Welcome to Guardian Mt. Hood, where the art of Jiu Jitsu is more than a practice—it's a way of life. Together, we grow stronger, smarter, and more resilient, always striving to be warriors in the garden of life.

Note to Parents

Dear Parents,

At our academy, we aim to nurture not only your child's martial arts skills but also their personal growth. We place a strong emphasis on the concept of "Blackbelt Effort": giving your best in every situation and never giving up, no matter how challenging it may be. This effort extends beyond Brazilian Jiu Jitsu and into their daily lives—at home, in school, and within the community.

To reinforce this philosophy, we encourage open communication between parents, coaches, and students. Together, we can help your child practice Blackbelt Effort both on and off the mat. We will celebrate and reward students who display this effort in all areas of life. However, if a student is not meeting expectations, such as giving their best effort during practice, there may be consequences like a loss of sparring time to reinforce accountability and learning.

Please feel free to reach out to us at any time. We are here to support both you and your child in their journey to success in martial arts and life.

Sincerely,
In peace and progress,
Professor Jose and Coach Angelica
Guardian Mt. Hood Brazilian Jiu Jitsu

Students,

I hope this handbook finds you all in good health and high spirits, both on and off the mats. As we continue our journey together in Brazilian Jiu Jitsu, I want to take a moment to address a very important topic that is often overlooked in the heat of training: injury prevention.

One of the greatest things about BJJ is that it can be practiced for a lifetime, but in order to keep training and progressing, we need to protect ourselves and each other from unnecessary injuries. This sport is not just about building physical strength, but also about cultivating a strong mind, learning control, and leaving our egos outside the gym. By taking a mindful approach to your training, you can enjoy the benefits of BJJ without sidelining yourself due to preventable injuries.

You Are Your Best Measure of Safety

The reality is that you are your best defense when it comes to injury prevention. No one knows your body better than you do, so it's important to listen to it and act accordingly. Let's discuss a few principles that will help you stay safe while still progressing and enjoying your training:

1. Tap Early, Tap Often

The beauty of BJJ is that it allows us to test ourselves in a safe environment, but that safety depends on respecting the tap. The tap is your way of telling your training partner (and yourself) that the technique has worked and the fight is over.

There is no shame in tapping. In fact, it's the smart and responsible thing to do. Waiting until the last moment or trying to power out of submissions can lead to serious injuries—especially to the joints, which can be slow to heal.

Tap early and tap often. If you feel caught, don't let your ego stop you from tapping. Every tap is an opportunity to learn and improve. We all want to roll tomorrow, next week, and for many years to come.

2. Leave Your Ego Outside the Gym

Ego is the biggest enemy of progress and safety. When you let ego dictate your training, you'll push beyond your limits, make bad decisions, and risk injury. Whether you're a white belt or a higher belt, remember:

BJJ is about learning, not winning. Trying to "win" every roll can lead to dangerous decisions, both for you and your training partners.

Respect the learning process. Don't be afraid to slow down, ask questions, and embrace the small losses that teach you so much. True progress comes from being humble and curious, not from trying to prove something.

3. Don't Be Afraid to Say "No"

Sometimes, it's okay to turn down a roll or choose your training partners carefully. If you ever feel unsafe or uncomfortable rolling with someone—whether they are too aggressive, too unpredictable, or simply out of sync with your style or pace—don't hesitate to sit out or politely decline the roll.

Your safety comes first. Never feel pressured to roll with someone who puts you in unsafe positions or who trains recklessly. There is no shame in protecting yourself.

Communicate with your partners. Let them know if you have any injuries or areas of concern before starting a roll. A good training partner will always respect your boundaries.

4. Recognize When to Rest

As much as we all love training, it's important to recognize when your body needs rest. Overtraining can lead to fatigue, poor decisionmaking, and injuries. Listen to your body—if you're feeling pain, soreness, or general burnout, give yourself permission to take a day off or scale back your intensity.

Rest is part of the process. Recovery is as important as training. You'll come back stronger and more focused when you give your body the time it needs to heal and recharge.

Training smart is better than training hard. Know your limits and recognize when to rest or dial back the intensity. This mindset will ensure longevity in the sport.

5. Be a Good Training Partner

We are all responsible for keeping each other safe on the mats. When you train with others, it's important to remember that we all have different goals, experience levels, and physical abilities. Approach every roll with respect, awareness, and control.

Check your intensity. It's okay to roll hard when both partners agree to it, but make sure you're always in control. Don't crank submissions or use brute strength—this can lead to injuries.

Be aware of your partner's skill level and physical limits. Adjust your rolling intensity accordingly, and prioritize technique over force.

6. Warm Up Properly

Injury prevention starts even before you step onto the mat. A proper warmup will help increase blood flow to your muscles, loosen up your joints, and prepare your body for the demands of BJJ.

Never skip the warmup. Whether it's drilling, stretching, or light rolling, your body needs this time to prepare for more intense activity.

Take your time. Stretching and mobility work should be a regular part of your routine, especially if you notice stiffness or pain in certain areas.

Final Thoughts

BJJ is a journey that we're all on together. By focusing on smart, safe training, we can ensure that this journey is long, fulfilling, and injury free. Please remember: tapping early, leaving your ego at the door, and making thoughtful decisions about your training partners are key to staying safe and healthy. Let's continue to look out for each other, train mindfully, and keep the mats a positive and safe environment for everyone.

If you ever feel unsure or need guidance, don't hesitate to reach out to your instructors or teammates. We are all here to support each other.

Train safe, train smart, and I'll see you on the mats!

<h1 style="text-align:center">Resources for Training Outside of Class: A Balanced Approach</h1>

Brazilian Jiu Jitsu (BJJ) is a journey that extends far beyond the mats of our academy. Many of you are eager to continue learning and exploring outside of class time, which is fantastic! There are countless resources available today, such as cross training in other martial arts, YouTube tutorials, social media, and seminars. These can provide valuable insights and help you grow in BJJ, but they must be approached with caution and responsibility. The choices you make in seeking out additional training resources don't just affect you—they also impact your teammates, who may not be familiar with certain techniques or who rely on you being injury free to continue their own development.

Let's dive into these resources, reviewing the pros and cons of each, and how to responsibly incorporate them into your training while keeping yourself and your teammates safe.

1. Cross Training in Other Martial Arts

Cross training in other martial arts—such as wrestling, judo, or striking disciplines like Muay Thai—can improve specific aspects of your BJJ game, especially in takedowns, balance, and overall physicality. However, there are some key considerations to keep in mind.

Pros:
 Improved Takedowns and Defense: Wrestling or judo can enhance your ability to control opponents during standup exchanges, and give you new tools for offense and defense.
 Broader Skill Set: Cross training can expose you to a wide range of techniques, making you a more well-rounded martial artist.
 Fitness Benefits: Additional training can improve your cardio, strength, and conditioning, which translates into better performance on the mats.

Cons:
 Risk of Injury: Wrestling and judo are highimpact arts that involve intense physicality and throws. These activities can increase your risk of injury, which will keep you off the mats and deprive your teammates of a valuable training partner.

 Conflicting Concepts: Different martial arts emphasize techniques that might contradict the principles of BJJ. Integrating them without proper guidance could lead to confusion and inefficiency, not just for you, but for your training partners who haven't learned to counter or defend these new movements.

Impact on Teammates:
Cross training can expose you to techniques that your BJJ teammates haven't learned or practiced defending against. For example, introducing highamplitude takedowns or explosive throws can pose a significant injury risk to someone who hasn't been trained to fall properly.

Always discuss new concepts with your coach before bringing them to the mat to ensure they can be safely integrated into training sessions.

2. YouTube Tutorials

YouTube has revolutionized how we learn BJJ, offering thousands of instructional videos that cover everything from basic techniques to advanced submissions. While this can be a great supplement to your training, it comes with important caveats.

Pros:
Access to a Wide Range of Techniques: You can explore new submissions, escapes, or passing strategies you may not have covered yet in class.

Free Learning Resource: It's a cost effective way to learn new moves and expand your knowledge base.

Immediate Help: You can quickly find answers or refreshers on techniques you're currently working on in class.

Cons:
Information Overload: With so much content available, it's easy to get overwhelmed or distracted by techniques that don't fit your current level or game.

No Feedback or Context: YouTube videos lack the personal touch and realtime feedback of a coach, which can lead to practicing techniques incorrectly or dangerously.

Questionable Sources: Not all content is made by reputable instructors, and you may unknowingly incorporate flawed or risky techniques into your game.

Impact on Teammates:
When you bring new techniques from YouTube into sparring or drilling, remember that your teammates might not be familiar with how to defend against them or recognize the danger signs of certain submissions. For example, submissions like leg locks can be particularly dangerous if improperly applied or defended. If a teammate is caught off guard by a technique they haven't seen before, it increases the likelihood of injury. Always consult your coach before introducing new techniques to make sure they're appropriate for your current level and safe for everyone involved.

3. Social Media and BJJ Forums

Social media platforms like Instagram, Facebook, and BJJ forums offer an enormous amount of content, from technique videos to competition footage and discussions on BJJ philosophy. These platforms are great for staying engaged with the global BJJ community but can also present risks if approached irresponsibly.

Pros:
Staying Motivated and Connected: Following high level practitioners and being part of online discussions can keep you motivated and expose you to new ideas.

Learning from Elite Competitors: Many toplevel competitors and black belts share valuable insights and breakdowns that can inspire and inform your training.

Access to Training Tips: Social media allows you to see how others are drilling, training, and competing, offering inspiration and new drills or techniques to try.

Cons:
Overemphasis on Flashy Moves: Social media tends to highlight advanced, flashy techniques that may not be suitable for your current skill level. Trying these without understanding the underlying fundamentals can lead to injuries.

Comparison Trap: Constantly comparing yourself to elitelevel athletes can be demotivating and make you feel like you're not progressing quickly enough.

Unfiltered Advice: Not all advice you find in forums or comments is reliable or suitable for your progression. Implementing advice without consulting your coach can lead to setbacks.

Impact on Teammates:
Social media often glamorizes high risk techniques or advanced submissions that may not be appropriate for your level or for your training partners. Introducing flashy moves in sparring without understanding the risk could put your teammates at a disadvantage, especially if they are unfamiliar with how to defend or counter these techniques. This increases the risk of injury, which affects not just the injured person but also the entire team dynamic. Injuries reduce the number of training partners available to the rest of the class, disrupting the learning environment.

4. BJJ Seminars

Seminars are a fantastic way to learn from worldclass instructors and expose yourself to techniques that are outside your regular curriculum. They offer deep dives into specific areas of BJJ, which can accelerate your understanding of certain positions or concepts.

Pros:

Access to Elite Instruction: Seminars give you the opportunity to learn directly from some of the best in the world, often providing unique insights or techniques.

Focused Learning: Seminars often concentrate on a particular position, submission, or concept, which allows for a deeper understanding of that topic.

Networking Opportunities: Seminars connect you with other practitioners and broaden your BJJ network, both locally and internationally.

Cons:

Overwhelming Amount of Information: Seminars can cover a lot of material in a short time, which can make it difficult to absorb everything and apply it effectively.

Techniques May Not Fit Your Current Level: The advanced techniques or strategies shared in seminars may be challenging to incorporate into your game, especially if they are far beyond what you've learned so far.

Cost: Seminars can be pricey, and without proper integration, you might not get the full value from the experience.

Impact on Teammates:

When returning from a seminar, it's tempting to immediately apply the new techniques you've learned. However, your teammates may not have the same understanding of these new moves, particularly if they involve advanced submissions or complex positions. This can lead to confusion, frustration, or even injuries if not introduced properly. Before trying out seminar techniques in sparring, share them with your coach to see how they can be safely incorporated into class drills or situational training. This ensures your teammates are introduced to the new concepts in a structured and safe way.

Conclusion: Use Outside Resources Responsibly

It's important to remember that outside resources are meant to enhance, not replace, your core training at the academy. Whether it's cross training, YouTube, social media, or seminars, each of these resources has great potential to benefit your development, but they also come with risks—not just for you, but for your teammates. Injuries disrupt the learning environment, not only for you but for the entire class, as injured teammates won't be able to train and contribute to the team's collective growth.

Always prioritize communication with your coach before incorporating new techniques or approaches into your game. Your instructor can help guide you on how to integrate what you've learned in a way that's safe for you and beneficial for the entire team. Remember, Brazilian Jiu

Jitsu is a team sport, and keeping yourself and your teammates healthy and injuryfree is critical to everyone's progress and enjoyment of the art.

Train smart, train safe, and I'll see you on the mats!

Brazilian Jiu Jitsu Etiquette and Considerations for a Respectful and Safe Training Environment

Brazilian Jiu Jitsu (BJJ) is not just about physical technique; it's about fostering a respectful, inclusive, and safe environment where everyone—regardless of size, gender, or experience level—can learn and grow. Proper etiquette is essential to maintaining a positive atmosphere in the academy, both on and off the mats. Below are some key principles and guidelines to help you navigate training, rolling, and interactions with your teammates, including considerations for women, smaller or less experienced practitioners, and recognizing trauma triggers.

<h1 style="text-align:center">General BJJ Etiquette</h1>

1. Respect the Mat and Your Teammates:

Always bow or acknowledge the mat before stepping on. This shows respect for the space where you learn and train.

Keep your uniform (gi or nogi attire) clean, and personal hygiene should always be a priority—trimmed nails, clean feet, and fresh gear are nonnegotiable.

Show respect to everyone on the mat, regardless of rank. BJJ is built on mutual respect, and everyone is here to learn and grow.

2. Listen to Your Instructor:

Pay attention during class. When the instructor is demonstrating a technique, give them your full attention and refrain from talking or distracting others.

Follow class structure and drills as instructed, and avoid deviating from the lesson plan unless your coach gives permission.

3. Tap Early and Often:

Safety comes first. If you're caught in a submission, don't let pride or ego stop you from tapping. Your safety is more important than winning a round of sparring.

When applying submissions, always do so with control and be mindful of your training partner's safety.

Rolling with Women, Smaller, or Less Experienced Partners

Training with a diverse group of people is one of the best aspects of BJJ, as it teaches adaptability and respect for different body types, genders, and skill levels. However, it's important to approach each training partner with an understanding of how to roll in a way that fosters safety and learning for both parties.

1. Rolling with Women:

Respect and Awareness: Women may face different challenges on the mats due to size or gender dynamics. Always approach these rolls with respect, and avoid using excessive strength or aggression. BJJ is about technique, not overpowering your partner.

No Special Treatment, Just Respect: Don't assume a woman wants to be handled delicately, but also don't treat the roll as a competition to prove something. Communicate clearly—ask if they have any preferences or areas they're focusing on, and adjust your intensity accordingly.

Avoiding Awkward Situations: BJJ involves close physical contact. While this is part of the art, be aware of body positioning to avoid unnecessary awkwardness. If you're unsure about anything, just communicate. Open dialogue ensures both parties feel comfortable and respected.

2. Rolling with Smaller or Less Experienced Practitioners:

Control Your Strength: When rolling with smaller or less experienced partners, it's critical to use control and avoid muscling through techniques. These training sessions should be focused on developing technique rather than dominating your partner.

Be a Mentor, Not a Bully: As a more experienced or larger practitioner, your role is to help your partner improve, not to showcase your own abilities. Help them build confidence by allowing them to work through techniques and positions.

Keep Ego in Check: Remember, BJJ is a journey. Rolling hard against less experienced teammates won't benefit either party. Focus on sharpening your own technique and helping your partner learn in a safe environment.

3. Communication and Checking In:

Always ask your partner before you begin sparring if they have any injuries or specific things they are working on. This helps tailor the roll to their needs and keeps them safe.

If at any point during the roll you sense your partner is uncomfortable or struggling, ask if they're okay or need to adjust the pace. BJJ is about mutual benefit, and communication is key to a positive experience.

Recognizing and Addressing Trauma Triggers

BJJ, while incredibly beneficial, can also be physically and emotionally intense. For some, certain positions, physical contact, or moments of perceived helplessness may trigger emotional or trauma related responses. It's important to recognize and be mindful of this in yourself and others.

1. What Are Trauma Triggers?

Trauma triggers are emotional reactions caused by a reminder of a past traumatic event. In BJJ, close physical contact, being pinned or held down, or certain positions (e.g., back control or being mounted) may cause someone to feel anxiety, panic, or distress.

2. Recognizing Triggers in Yourself and Others:

For Yourself: If you find certain positions or situations triggering, it's crucial to communicate this to your training partner or instructor. You can ask to avoid certain positions or scenarios, or even take a break when needed. Your mental wellbeing is just as important as your physical safety.

For Others: If you notice a training partner seems distressed—whether they freeze up, become highly anxious, or appear uncomfortable in certain positions—pause the roll and ask if they're okay. Respect their boundaries and offer to modify the intensity or position if needed.

3. How to Address Triggers:

Communication is Key: Always encourage open dialogue with your training partners. If someone shares that they have experienced trauma or prefers not to engage in certain positions, honor that request with full respect.

Pace and Space: Be aware of the pace at which you are rolling and give your partner space if they need to reset or regain composure. Don't rush or force the situation.

Respect Personal Boundaries: If someone needs to stop or take a break, let them. They may need to step off the mats to regulate their emotions or simply need to slow down the intensity of the roll.

Final Thoughts on Etiquette, Safety, and Respect

At the end of the day, BJJ is a practice built on respect, humility, and camaraderie. When you step onto the mat, you are responsible not just for your own safety and growth, but for that of your teammates as well. Whether you're rolling with women, smaller or less experienced practitioners, or someone who may be managing trauma, your role is to ensure a safe, respectful, and inclusive environment for everyone.

Be mindful, stay open to communication, and always prioritize respect and empathy. This is how we build not only better martial artists but better teammates and individuals.

Expectations of belts

White: show up 2+ times a week with an open mind and enthusiasm to learn and patience when it seems like you're not. Develop your defense

Blue: Be a good teammate: not trying to beat everyone but make them better to make you better. Be a role model. Don't take submissions personal. Recognize they're lessons and be grateful. Take the great defense you have to create opportunities to develop an offense. Don't quit rounds, classes or competitions just because you're not doing well. Embrace those lessons for the next practice

Purple: utilizing all characteristics of the belts before take the great defense and offense you have now developed and intertwined them into a style. Sharpen your techniques by showing teammates how to beat them. Be a rocket when it's needed and a parachute when others need it.

Brown: Take the culmination of all the skills you have learned in the belts prior along with the mistakes you have made and reteach them to another. As you do so you relearn them all yourself.

Black: Start over! Be the representative of your school and your professors. Take their teachings and build up them while staying true to the foundation you acquired. Keep your skills sharp until time comes to take it.

For a white belt transitioning to blue belt in Brazilian Jiu Jitsu (BJJ), the focus should be on fundamental techniques, principles, and an understanding of basic positional control. While promotion criteria can vary from academy to academy, certain universal concepts are typically expected.

1. Foundational Concepts
   Positional Hierarchy: Understanding the concept of dominant positions (mount, side control, back control, guard, etc.) and how to move through them.
   Escapes: Ability to escape inferior positions like mount, side control, and back mount.
   Basic Submissions: Familiarity with a few key submissions such as the armbar, triangle choke, rear naked choke, kimura, and guillotine.
   Defense: Basic defenses against submissions, recognizing danger early, and protecting yourself effectively.
   Takedowns: Knowledge of simple takedowns like the single leg, double leg, and a few guard pulling techniques.

2. Positional Awareness and Control
   Guard Knowledge: A white belt should demonstrate a solid understanding of closed guard, basic open guard, and know how to maintain guard while understanding sweeps.
   Closed Guard: Basic sweeps (hip bump, scissor sweep, etc.) and simple submission setups (armbar, triangle, guillotine).
   Open Guard: Concepts like standing up in base, maintaining guard, and preventing guard passes.

Side Control: How to maintain side control, transition to better positions like mount, and apply basic submissions from side control (kimura, Americana).

Mount: Control and submissions (armbar, Americana) from mount. Understanding how to maintain mount without getting swept.

Back Control: Understanding of maintaining back control and executing submissions like the rear naked choke, as well as escape attempts.

3. Movement and Transitions

Shrimping: Effective shrimping to escape positions or create space.

Bridging: Using the bridge to escape mount or create movement.

Hip Movement: Proper use of the hips to escape, control, or transition positions.

4. Basic Drills and Concepts

Concept of Base: Keeping a stable base during sweeps, guard passes, and while defending submissions.

Rolling Etiquette: Rolling safely, controlling aggression, and being mindful of training partners.

Grips: Proper use of grips for control in both gi and nogi.

5. Submission Knowledge

Basic Attacks: Having a strong understanding of fundamental submissions from different positions.

Defense: Understanding when you're in danger, and being able to defend yourself intelligently (e.g., posture in guard to avoid submissions like the triangle or armbar).

6. Strategy and Mindset

Positional Escapes over Submissions: Emphasizing the importance of survival and escaping bad positions over focusing on submissions.

Patience: Developing the patience to apply techniques with control, rather than relying on strength and explosiveness.

Composure Under Pressure: Learning to stay calm and aware during rolling, especially in disadvantageous situations.

7. Overall Understanding

Basic Rules of BJJ: Understanding the general rules of BJJ competitions, what constitutes illegal techniques for their rank, and how to conduct oneself on the mat.

Growth Mindset: Demonstrating a willingness to learn, improve, and acknowledge mistakes.

8. Mat Time and Dedication

Consistency: Typically, a white belt will have logged a fair amount of mat time (often 1 to 2 years of training), which reflects their dedication and commitment to learning.

These elements create a solid foundation. A white belt ready for blue belt should not necessarily master all these techniques, but they should be proficient and demonstrate a good understanding of the concepts, along with the ability to apply them during live rolling. BJJ is also about growth and perseverance, and readiness for a blue belt comes with the ability to keep calm, be respectful, and exhibit steady improvement.

The transition from blue to purple belt in Brazilian Jiu Jitsu (BJJ) marks a significant leap in both technical knowledge and the ability to apply that knowledge dynamically in live situations. A purple belt is often seen as a serious practitioner with a deep understanding of techniques and an emerging ability to strategize and adapt on the fly. While individual academies may have variations, there are some general expectations for blue belts before progressing to purple belt.

1. Technical Proficiency and Breadth
   Expanded Guard Knowledge: At purple belt level, a deeper understanding of multiple guard systems is expected.
   Guard Variations: Proficiency in closed guard, open guard, De La Riva, spider guard, half guard, butterfly guard, and lasso guard.
   Guard Sweeps and Retention: Ability to not only retain guard but also set up sweeps and submissions effectively from a variety of guard positions.
   Advanced Submissions: Knowledge of more advanced submission chains and setups, as well as transitions between submissions. Examples include:
   Armbar Variations: Knowing armbar setups from guard, mount, and side control.
   Chokes: Mastery of multiple choke variations (loop choke, brabo/D'arce choke, lapel chokes, bow and arrow, etc.).
   Leg Locks: Introduction to leg locks (straight ankle lock, toe hold, knee bar) within the legal scope for purple belts in competition.
   Offensive and Defensive Cycles: Ability to chain techniques together (e.g., transitioning between guard passes, sweeps, and submissions fluidly).

2. Positional Mastery and Transitions
   Control and Pressure: A blue belt advancing to purple belt should have honed their ability to maintain and control dominant positions with consistent pressure.
   Side Control: A strong understanding of transitions between various forms of side control (knee on belly, northsouth, etc.) and the ability to apply pressure effectively.
   Mount: Mastery of mount control, transitions between mount, side control, and back control, and ability to maintain dominant positions.
   Back Control: Greater mastery of back attacks, including refined details for maintaining hooks and controlling the opponent's movement.

3. Defensive Competence
   Escapes from All Positions: A purple belt should have welldeveloped escapes from bad positions (mount, back control, side control), and these escapes should be efficient and effective under pressure.
   Submission Defense: Recognizing and defending submissions earlier and more efficiently, especially when facing advanced setups.
   Countering Takedowns and Guard Passing: More refined techniques for countering common guard passes and defending against takedowns or sweeps.

4. Guard Passing Proficiency

Multiple Passing Strategies: A purple belt should have a clear understanding of passing various types of guards (open, closed, spider, De La Riva, half guard, etc.).

Pressure Passes: Proficiency with pressurebased passes (over/under pass, knee slice, smash pass).

Speed Passes: Ability to execute speedbased passes (Toreando, Xpass, or leg drags).

Flow and Adaptation: Understanding when to transition between passing styles based on the opponent's defense and guard type.

5. Takedowns and Standup Skills

Expanded Takedown Knowledge: While BJJ often emphasizes ground fighting, a purple belt should demonstrate a broader knowledge of takedowns.

Judo Throws: Basic judo throws such as Ouchi Gari, Uchi Mata, and Osoto Gari.

Wrestling Takedowns: Refining wrestlingstyle takedowns like double leg, single leg, and ankle picks.

Guard Pulling with Purpose: Understanding when and how to pull guard effectively during sparring or competition.

6. Comprehensive Strategy and Flow

Strategic Thinking: A blue belt moving to purple should begin thinking in terms of game plans, strategies, and tactics, both for specific opponents and types of matches.

Positional Awareness: A growing ability to dictate the pace and position of a match by controlling grips, pressure, and transitions.

Anticipating Opponents' Moves: Developing the ability to anticipate an opponent's reactions and prepare counters in advance, both offensively and defensively.

7. Advanced Rolling Skills

Flow Rolling: The ability to roll with fluidity, transitioning from technique to technique without relying purely on strength. This shows not only an understanding of technique but the capability to apply it with finesse.

Submission Chains: Proficiency in chaining submissions together, anticipating when an opponent defends one technique and flowing into another.

Rolling with Purpose: The ability to roll not just for the sake of submissions but to explore techniques, learn from failures, and adapt to different body types and strategies.

8. Teaching and Mentorship

Helping Lower Belts: Purple belts are often seen as emerging leaders on the mats. A blue belt should demonstrate the ability to help and guide lower belts by explaining fundamental concepts and techniques.

Understanding Fundamentals Deeply: Part of progressing to purple is not just learning new techniques but refining the fundamentals so well that they can be taught and passed on to others.

9. Mat IQ and Competition Readiness

Competition Experience: While not mandatory, many practitioners aiming for purple belt gain experience in competition, showing that they can apply their skills under pressure.

Mat IQ: A blue belt transitioning to purple should have a growing understanding of the "game" of BJJ, recognizing opportunities to score points in competition, transitioning through positions smoothly, and maintaining composure in highstress situations.

10. Dedication and Consistency

Time and Training: Purple belt is often considered one of the most challenging belts to earn because it requires consistent time on the mats, often 35 years after earning the blue belt. Dedication to training, improving, and continuing to grow is key.

11. Character and Humility

BJJ Lifestyle: A purple belt often signifies someone deeply committed to the BJJ lifestyle, not just in terms of skill but in embodying the values of humility, respect, and continuous learning.

Dealing with Ego: By purple belt, practitioners should have a strong ability to manage their ego, recognize the value in both winning and losing, and approach training with a growth mindset.

A purple belt candidate should not only have technical skills but also demonstrate a well-rounded understanding of the art and a sense of purpose in their training. The journey from blue to purple requires not only deepening technical knowledge but also maturing as a practitioner in mindset, patience, and ability to teach and help others grow on the mats.

The transition from purple to brown belt in Brazilian Jiu Jitsu (BJJ) marks a significant shift from technical competence to mastery. By the time a practitioner reaches brown belt, they are approaching expert level and are expected to demonstrate a high level of skill, adaptability, and a deep understanding of the art. This phase is often about refining techniques, improving precision, and preparing for the eventual leap to black belt.

1. Technical Mastery

Refinement of Techniques: A brown belt should not only know a wide variety of techniques but also execute them with precision and efficiency. Techniques that may have been "rough" at purple belt should now be smooth, well timed, and purposeful.

Clean Execution: The key to the brown belt level is mastering the small details—grip adjustments, weight distribution, timing—that elevate technique from effective to near perfect.

Breadth of Knowledge: Brown belts are expected to have a well-rounded game, both offensively and defensively. This includes:

Strong Guard Systems: Proficiency in multiple advanced guard systems (e.g., Xguard, inverted guard, lapel guards, etc.), and the ability to attack or defend from various guards.

Dynamic Sweeps and Submissions: Ability to execute sweeps and submissions from a variety of positions and create fluid transitions between them.

Advanced Passing: Mastery of guard passing, including leg drags, pressure passing, and speedbased passing. Brown belts should pass the guard of lower belts consistently and handle advanced guard systems effectively.

2. Positional Control and Dominance

Tighter Control: A brown belt should show a level of control that demonstrates mastery over positions such as mount, side control, and back control. There is a focus on holding these positions against resistance while preparing to transition to submissions.

Transitions Between Dominant Positions: Fluidity in transitioning between positions without losing control. For example, moving from side control to mount, then to back control, while maintaining pressure and dominance.

Pressure and Weight Distribution: The ability to apply consistent pressure, forcing opponents into making mistakes. Brown belts understand how to use their body weight efficiently to control and fatigue their opponents.

3. Submission Mastery and Creativity

Submissions from Everywhere: A brown belt should be able to set up and execute submissions from virtually any position, with a particular emphasis on:

Submission Chains: Executing submissions in a sequence, transitioning between them fluidly (e.g., from triangle to armbar to omoplata).

Unorthodox Submissions: Mastery of less common submissions (e.g., wrist locks, loop chokes, rolling submissions) and the ability to improvise depending on the opponent's reactions.

Leg Locks: While still abiding by legal restrictions for brown belts, leg lock knowledge should be solid, particularly with straight ankle locks and toe holds. Many academies also introduce advanced leg lock systems at this level, although heel hooks may still be limited by competition rules.

4. Guard Mastery and Retention

Advanced Guard Retention: A brown belt is expected to defend and retain their guard against high level opponents, not just by using individual techniques but by understanding guard retention concepts deeply.

Guard Play: Proficiency in both offensive and defensive guard play, with the ability to dictate the pace from the bottom. A brown belt should be able to sweep, submit, or recover from virtually any guard position.

5. Advanced Takedowns and Standup Game

Takedown Mastery: At brown belt, takedowns become more refined. Brown belts should be proficient in judo and wrestling style takedowns, including:

Throws and Trips: Mastery of basic and advanced judo throws (e.g., Uchi Mata, Seoi Nage) and foot sweeps.

Wrestling Takedowns: Effective use of single leg and double leg takedowns, especially against resisting opponents.

Defense Against Takedowns: Ability to counter and sprawl effectively, maintaining balance and avoiding takedown attempts.

6. Strategy and Game Planning

Strategic Mindset: A brown belt should not just be reactive but should proactively implement strategies, demonstrating a high level of "mat IQ" during sparring or competition. This includes:

Imposing Game Plans: Developing the ability to dictate the flow of a match based on a specific game plan (e.g., pulling guard to set up sweeps or takedowns to lead into passing).

Adaptability: Understanding when to change strategies mid match if something isn't working. A brown belt should be able to adapt and adjust without hesitation, blending different styles seamlessly.

Point Awareness in Competition: In competition, brown belts should be acutely aware of the points system and how to capitalize on it to control and win matches.

7. Defensive Mastery

Escape Mastery: Brown belts should have extremely well honed escapes, able to free themselves from bad positions quickly and efficiently.

Advanced Submission Defense: Recognizing and defending against even the most advanced submissions, such as rolling chokes, leg locks, and complex joint locks, early and effectively.

Positional Escapes: Ability to escape from the worst positions (e.g., mount, back control) consistently, using both technique and strategic awareness.

8. Teaching and Mentorship

Leadership Role on the Mat: Brown belts often take on leadership roles within the academy, assisting with teaching lower belts and providing detailed feedback. They should be able to explain complex concepts clearly and help guide less experienced practitioners.

Technical Teaching: Not only knowing the techniques but having the ability to break them down and teach them effectively, showing a deeper level of understanding.

Mentorship: Acting as a mentor for blue and purple belts, helping them grow not just technically but in their overall approach to BJJ.

Responsibility in Sparring: Demonstrating responsibility during live rolling, particularly when sparring with lower belts, showing control and an understanding of how to roll safely without injuring others.

9. Competition Performance

High level Competition: Many brown belts will have extensive competition experience and should be able to perform well against high level opponents. Their ability to strategize, adapt, and impose their game plan under pressure is tested and refined in this environment.

Composure Under Pressure: A brown belt demonstrates composure in difficult situations, knowing when to be patient and when to attack, even under the stress of competition.

10. Character and Philosophy

Mastery of Ego: By the time a practitioner reaches brown belt, their ego should be well under control. The focus is on learning, teaching, and improving, rather than on "winning" rolls. Humility is expected.

Contribution to the Academy: A brown belt is expected to contribute positively to the academy's culture, promoting values like respect, discipline, and camaraderie among teammates.

Internal Growth: At this stage, the journey is as much about internal growth as it is about technical mastery. The practitioner should exhibit a deep sense of self awareness, growth, and commitment to the art.

11. Preparation for Black Belt

Self-Reflection: A brown belt should begin to reflect deeply on their journey, understanding not only the technical aspects but the philosophical and personal development aspects of BJJ.

Filling in the Gaps: Brown belts are expected to identify weaknesses in their game and focus on filling those gaps. This often involves perfecting their techniques and refining aspects of their style that need improvement before reaching black belt.

Readiness for Black Belt: A brown belt should begin to show signs of black belt readiness, which includes not only technical mastery but embodying the values of a black belt—leadership, respect, humility, and the desire to give back to the community.

In summary, the transition from purple to brown belt involves refining all areas of a practitioner's game, mastering not only individual techniques but the entire flow of Brazilian Jiu Jitsu. The focus at this level shifts from accumulating knowledge to perfecting and polishing one's understanding of the art, teaching others, and embodying the core values of BJJ both on and off the mat. The brown belt represents a culmination of years of dedication, preparing the practitioner for the final leap to black belt, where the journey of mastery continues.

The journey from brown to black belt in Brazilian Jiu Jitsu (BJJ) is the culmination of years, sometimes decades, of hard work, dedication, and personal growth. By the time a practitioner reaches black belt, they are not only expected to have mastered the technical aspects of the art but also to embody the philosophy and spirit of BJJ both on and off the mat. The progression from brown to black is often seen as refining the final details, while also developing leadership qualities, humility, and the ability to give back to the BJJ community. Let's explore the key areas of development expected for a brown belt advancing to black.

1. Technical Mastery

Flawless Execution: A brown belt transitioning to black should be able to execute techniques with near perfect precision. This includes everything from basic movements to the most advanced submissions, transitions, and positional controls.

Efficiency: Black belts are expected to perform techniques with minimal wasted effort, maximizing efficiency in both offense and defense.

Mastery of Fundamentals: While advanced techniques are important, black belts should have a deep, almost instinctual mastery of the fundamentals. These basics become the cornerstone of their game, executed at the highest level.

Personal Game Development: By black belt, a practitioner has likely developed a personal game—a set of strategies, techniques, and positions that work best for their body type, mindset, and style of fighting. This game is honed to perfection.

Adaptability and Creativity: Black belts should demonstrate a deep ability to adapt to any situation or opponent. They must be able to think on their feet and react creatively when faced with unexpected challenges.

2. Positional Mastery and Control

Flawless Positional Control: A black belt demonstrates a level of control that seems effortless. They can hold dominant positions (mount, side control, back control) even against skilled opponents, using minimal energy.

Transitions: Transitions between positions are fluid, and a black belt can maintain dominance while moving seamlessly between side control, mount, and back control. They also know when to yield positions strategically.

Understanding of Weight and Pressure: Mastery of using body weight and pressure to control an opponent is a hallmark of black belt level, where every movement serves a purpose in maintaining control or advancing position.

3. Submission Mastery

Effortless Submissions: Black belts apply submissions with precision and fluidity. They should be able to set up and execute submissions from any position, often using subtle adjustments to finish techniques that appear inevitable.

Submission Chains: Advanced chaining of submissions is expected at this level, where an opponent's defense only leads to a different, equally effective attack.

High Level Finishing Mechanics: A black belt has perfected the finishing mechanics of submissions. Whether it's an armbar, choke, or leg lock, a black belt's submission attempts are efficient, calculated, and effective.

4. Defense and Escapes

Impeccable Defense: A black belt should have nearly impenetrable defense, being able to survive and escape even the worst positions or submission attempts with grace.

Calm Under Pressure: Black belts maintain composure in the most challenging situations, showing a calm and calculated approach to defending against high level attacks.

Escape Sequences: Escapes are not desperate movements but planned sequences. Black belts know exactly how to escape from mount, side control, and back control with minimal effort, often reversing the situation into a favorable position.

5. Takedowns and Standup Proficiency

Complete Takedown Game: While BJJ emphasizes ground fighting, a black belt is expected to have a well rounded takedown game, including proficiency in judo and wrestling techniques.

Takedown Setups: Black belts can set up takedowns using grips, footwork, and timing, whether it's a judo throw, single leg, or double leg takedown.

Standup Defense: Defense against takedowns is equally important. A black belt should be adept at sprawling, grip fighting, and countering takedown attempts.

6. Teaching and Mentorship

Leadership on the Mat: Black belts are natural leaders, not only because of their rank but because they carry the responsibility of passing on the knowledge they've gained. They are expected to mentor lower belts and provide guidance both in and out of class.

Technical Teaching: Black belts should be able to break down complex techniques and explain them in a way that's accessible to students of all levels. This shows a deep understanding of the art.

Encouraging Growth in Others: As mentors, black belts inspire others to improve, guiding students through their own BJJ journeys and helping them overcome plateaus or challenges.

7. Strategic Understanding and Mat IQ

Mastery of Strategy: By the time a practitioner reaches black belt, they should have a profound understanding of BJJ strategy. This includes recognizing patterns in opponents' movements, anticipating attacks, and capitalizing on weaknesses.

Game Planning: Black belts should be able to create and execute game plans during competition or rolling, adapting their approach based on the specific strengths and weaknesses of their opponent.

Adaptation and Counter play: A black belt doesn't just react to what their opponent does—they anticipate, adapt, and counter long before the opponent completes their move. This level of "mat IQ" reflects a deep mental game.

8. Competition and Testing

High level Competition: While competition is not mandatory for black belt promotion, many practitioners reach black belt after proving themselves in competition. Black belts should be able to perform under pressure and exhibit a composed and strategic approach to both gi and nogi competitions.

Mindset in Competition: Black belts demonstrate calmness, focus, and the ability to maintain their game plan under the most stressful conditions.

Consistency: At this level, consistency is key—black belts perform well not just occasionally but across multiple matches, whether in competition or daily rolling.

9. Philosophy and Growth Mindset

Continual Learning: Reaching black belt is not the end of the journey—it's often described as the beginning of true mastery. Black belts are expected to maintain a growth mindset, continuing to learn, refine their game, and remain open to new ideas and techniques.

Humility: A true black belt embodies humility, recognizing that despite their rank, there is always more to learn. They remain students of the art, constantly seeking improvement.

Philosophical Depth: Black belts often develop a philosophical understanding of BJJ and life. They've come to understand that the lessons learned on the mat—discipline, perseverance, humility—apply to all aspects of life.

10. Character and Responsibility

Representing the Art: Black belts carry the responsibility of representing the art of BJJ with integrity, humility, and respect. They should be role models for their teammates, students, and the larger BJJ community.

Ego Control: By this stage, ego is no longer a driving force. Black belts roll with a sense of purpose, helping others grow while continuing their own journey of self-improvement.

Service to the Community: Black belts often feel a responsibility to give back to the BJJ community, whether by teaching, mentoring, or contributing to the growth of the sport through seminars, competitions, or simply by leading by example.

11. Self-Mastery and Reflection

Inner Peace and Composure: Black belts are expected to have reached a level of self-mastery, not only in their technical abilities but in their mental and emotional control. They demonstrate poise and confidence but without arrogance.

Reflection on the Journey: By the time a practitioner reaches black belt, they've likely faced significant challenges—injuries, setbacks, plateaus. A black belt reflects on these experiences and grows from them, using the lessons learned to teach and inspire others.

Legacy and Impact: Many black belts begin to think about the legacy they will leave behind. Whether it's through their students, contributions to the art, or personal philosophy, black belts are aware of the impact they have on the BJJ community and beyond.

Final Thoughts

The transition from brown to black belt is about refinement, mastery, and embodying the essence of Brazilian Jiu Jitsu. It's not just about technical prowess; it's about becoming a leader, teacher, and role model. A black belt should possess a deep understanding of BJJ, have an open mind for continuous growth, and uphold the values of respect, discipline, and humility. It marks the beginning of a new journey, where learning never truly ends, and the path to self-mastery continues.

The transition from black belt to coral belt in Brazilian Jiu Jitsu (BJJ) represents an extraordinary achievement, not just in terms of technical mastery but in lifelong dedication to the art. While the black belt is a significant milestone, the coral belt (comprising red and black belt and eventually red and white belt) is a testament to decades of teaching, contributing to the community, and continuing to evolve as both a practitioner and a mentor. This phase is less about learning new techniques and more about embodying and preserving the art, culture, and philosophy of BJJ.

Here's a breakdown of what is expected and what defines the journey from black belt to coral belt:

1. Time and Dedication

Longevity in the Art: One of the most defining aspects of reaching the coral belt is the amount of time spent in BJJ. Typically, it takes a minimum of 31 years from the time one receives their black belt to be eligible for the red and black coral belt. This timeframe reflects not only technical growth but a lifetime of contribution and commitment.

10 years as a Black Belt: To become eligible for the 6thdegree black belt (the first coral belt rank, red and black), a black belt practitioner must spend at least a decade training, teaching, and contributing to BJJ after receiving their black belt.

Continued Training and Engagement: While some might slow down physically due to aging, the expectation is that a coral belt continues to train, teach, and evolve in the art. Many coral belts maintain active participation in the community.

2. Preservation of BJJ

Custodians of the Art: Coral belts serve as gatekeepers and custodians of Brazilian Jiu Jitsu's traditions, values, and evolution. Their role is not only to preserve the technical aspects of BJJ but also to maintain and pass on its philosophies and ethos.

Legacy of Technique: Coral belts often become known for particular innovations or contributions to the art. This could be the development of certain guard systems, submissions, or approaches to teaching that have influenced the sport on a global scale.

Passing on Knowledge: The teaching role of a coral belt is critical. They are expected to train generations of black belts, ensuring that the art remains vibrant and that the standards of BJJ are upheld.

3. Mastery of the Art

Subtle Mastery: By the time someone reaches coral belt, their technical mastery of BJJ is expected to be profound, but it often manifests in subtle, refined movements that come from decades of practice.

Flawless Understanding of Fundamentals: While black belts may focus on advanced techniques, coral belts have a deep, intuitive understanding of the fundamentals, applying them with effortless precision.

Anticipation and Flow: Coral belts are often seen as being several steps ahead of their opponent, not through brute force or athleticism, but through a lifetime of experience that allows them to anticipate and neutralize attacks before they develop.

4. Philosophical Depth

Embodiment of BJJ Philosophy: At this stage, BJJ is no longer just a martial art but a way of life. Coral belts typically embody the highest philosophical aspects of BJJ, such as humility, perseverance, respect, and lifelong learning.

Teaching Through Philosophy: Coral belts are known for imparting wisdom not only about techniques but about life. They teach lessons that go beyond the mat, helping students apply the principles of BJJ—such as patience, adaptability, and resilience—to their everyday lives.

Humility and Responsibility: The ego, often battled and tempered throughout one's early BJJ journey, is expected to be entirely subdued by the time someone reaches coral belt. They understand their position as leaders and exemplify humility in everything they do.

5. Contribution to the BJJ Community

Influence and Impact: Coral belts are often seen as pillars of the global BJJ community. They are responsible for spreading the art, developing its culture, and ensuring that future generations have the opportunity to learn and train in an authentic and rigorous environment.

Running an Academy or Affiliation: Most coral belts have been involved in the creation or development of academies, affiliations, or organizations that play a significant role in the promotion of BJJ.

Mentorship of Black Belts: One of the coral belt's primary roles is the mentorship of black belts. They are responsible for guiding the next generation of instructors and practitioners, ensuring that the art continues to evolve while respecting its roots.

6. Leadership and Stewardship

Guardians of Tradition and Innovation: While coral belts respect the traditions of BJJ, they also recognize the importance of innovation. Many coral belts are responsible for adapting BJJ to new challenges, such as changes in competition rules, nogi advancements, and the global evolution of the sport.

Influence on the Sport: Coral belts frequently contribute to the evolution of BJJ's competitive ruleset and often serve in leadership roles within major BJJ organizations such as the IBJJF or other governing bodies.

Promotion of High Standards: Coral belts are known for setting high standards within their academies and associations, ensuring that the integrity of BJJ is preserved. They are responsible for promoting students through the belt system and ensuring that black belts under them continue to grow and maintain the highest levels of proficiency.

7. Teaching and Mentorship

Master Instructors: Coral belts are regarded as master instructors. They are not only teachers of technique but also teachers of teachers. They know how to communicate complex ideas simply and can adapt their teaching to different students' needs.

Dedication to Teaching: Coral belts often devote the majority of their time to teaching, and their methods are typically characterized by a depth of understanding, patience, and an ability to convey intricate details that only decades of practice can reveal.

Passing on BJJ's Values: Beyond technique, coral belts are tasked with imparting the core values of BJJ—such as respect, perseverance, and humility—to their students, ensuring that these principles remain central to the practice.

8. Authority and Recognition

Global Recognition: A coral belt is universally recognized and respected within the BJJ community as a senior authority. Their opinions on techniques, philosophy, and the direction of the sport are often sought after and carry significant weight.

A Source of Wisdom: Beyond technical expertise, coral belts are seen as sources of wisdom in both BJJ and life. Their decades of experience give them unique insights into training, competition, and personal growth, making them invaluable resources for both students and peers.

9. Physical Adaptation

Adapting to Age: While coral belts might not maintain the same level of physical performance as they did in their younger years, they adapt their game to suit their bodies, using leverage, timing, and technique to compensate for the natural decline in physical abilities.

Longevity and Health: Coral belts often serve as examples of how BJJ can be practiced for a lifetime. Many coral belts focus on maintaining their health and fitness to continue practicing well into their later years, promoting a sustainable approach to training.

10. The Transition to Red and White Belt

Preparation for the Final Phase: The next stage after the red and black coral belt is the red and white belt, which represents an even higher degree of mastery. It takes a minimum of seven additional years at the red and black belt level to be eligible for red and white. This belt signifies even deeper responsibility for the art's future.

Refinement of Mastery: A red and white belt represents further refinement of the qualities achieved at the red and black level. The focus shifts more toward mentorship, legacy building, and maintaining the highest ethical standards in the community.

Belt Expectations & Progression

White Belt:
Expectation: Show up with an open mind, energy, and a positive attitude at least twice a week. At this level, students are expected to focus on developing their defense and learning how to protect themselves, even when it seems challenging.
Blackbelt Effort: Consistently attend class and demonstrate a strong willingness to learn. Keep a good attitude, especially when things are tough or progress feels slow. Effort, not perfection, is key at this stage.

Grey Belt:
Expectation: Be a good teammate by helping others improve. Focus on learning from every round, whether you win or lose. At this level, continue building your defense and start looking for chances to apply offense. Understand that mistakes and submissions are opportunities to learn.
Blackbelt Effort: Don't give up when things get hard, whether in class or competitions. Instead, embrace the lessons that come from failure. Be resilient, patient, and always willing to try again.

Yellow Belt:
Expectation: Begin integrating what you've learned about defense and offense to develop your personal style. Teach others how to overcome your techniques, because by helping others, you refine your skills. Learn to adjust your intensity based on the situation, being fast and strong when needed but supportive and controlled when helping others.
Blackbelt Effort: Show leadership by setting a positive example for younger students. Be consistent in your training and approach each lesson as an opportunity to learn and improve. Understand that effort is about both giving and receiving knowledge.

Orange Belt:
Expectation: Refine everything you have learned up to this point. Take the experiences, mistakes, and lessons from earlier belts and use them to sharpen your skills. Focus on polishing your techniques and helping others develop theirs.
Blackbelt Effort: Lead by character, not just by skill. Stay humble and help your teammates grow, demonstrating patience and integrity. Apply effort not only in training but in life outside the academy, showing discipline, respect, and kindness.

Green Belt:
Expectation: At this level, it's about perfecting what you've learned while continuing to challenge yourself. Represent your school and your coaches by embodying the core values you've been taught. Your goal is to maintain the solid foundation you've built while pushing your limits as you prepare for leadership roles in the academy.
Blackbelt Effort: Continue to lead by example in all areas of your life. Embrace every opportunity to learn, teach, and grow. Stay humble, and understand that the journey of learning never ends, no matter your belt.

Conclusion

The belt progression in Brazilian Jiu Jitsu is not just about technical development but also about character growth. The concept of Blackbelt Effort encourages students to give their best in every situation, both on and off the mat. We aim to create a supportive environment where children can thrive, learning not only martial arts but also life skills that will shape them into responsible, respectful, and resilient individuals.

Together, we can help your child succeed and become the best version of themselves. Thank you for your continued support in this journey.

This curriculum is now tailored for youth students, with an emphasis on effort, personal growth, and leadership as they progress through each belt level.

This curriculum integrates the development of essential skills, techniques, and values expected for children at each stage, blending the multiple grey belt levels into a comprehensive learning track.

Core Concepts from White to Grey Belt (All Levels)

Fundamental Goals:
  Build a solid foundation of movement, control, and basic techniques.
  Emphasize safety, respect, and sportsmanship.
  Ensure the learning process is enjoyable, instilling a love for Brazilian Jiu Jitsu.
  Develop discipline, resilience, and teamwork through structured practice.

White Belt to Grey Belt Curriculum

1. Basic Movements and Body Awareness (Across All Levels)

At the beginning of their journey, children should focus on mastering basic movements that will be the building blocks of all future techniques:

Shrimping (Hip Escapes): Vital for guard recovery and movement on the ground.
Bridging and Rolling (Upa): Essential for escaping from bottom positions like mount.
Technical StandUp: A fundamental skill for returning to a standing position safely.
Forward and Backward Rolls: Develop agility, coordination, and body control.
Base and Balance Drills: Learning how to move with stability and control.

2. Key Positions and Escapes (Developing Positional Awareness)

As students progress from white to grey belt, understanding the various positions and their escapes is crucial. Below is the progression for key positions:

Mount:

Understanding top and bottom mount.
Top Mount: Basic control techniques, maintaining base, transitioning to submissions.
Bottom Mount: Escapes like trap and roll (upa) and elbow escapes (shrimping to guard).

Guard (Top and Bottom):
Closed Guard: Basics of maintaining closed guard, breaking posture, and setting up simple submissions and sweeps.
Guard Passing: Introduction to basic guard passes (standing guard break, knee slice pass).
Open Guard Concepts: Introduction to keeping distance with feet (feet on hips, butterfly hooks).

Side Control:
Top Side Control: Understanding the control and pressure needed to pin opponents.
Bottom Side Control: Simple hip escapes to recover guard or transition to a safer position.

Back Control:
Importance of maintaining back control (keeping hooks, seatbelt grip).
Basic escapes from back control (turning into the guard, escaping hooks).

3. Submissions and Submission Defense (Introduction and Refinement)

Children will be introduced to a range of basic submissions, with the emphasis placed on correct technique rather than force. Defense and the importance of tapping early will also be instilled.

Key Submissions:
Americana (Keylock): From mount and side control.
Armbar: From mount and guard (focus on mechanics, not pressure).
Triangle Choke: From closed guard (basic mechanics of positioning legs, without full pressure).
Rear Naked Choke (RNC): Understanding positioning without fully applying pressure.

Submission Defense:
Basic posture and grip breaking.
Defending against simple submissions like armbar and triangle.

4. Sweeps and Transitions (Learning to Change Positions)

As children move through the grey belt variations, they will be expected to demonstrate their ability to transition between positions, not just hold them.

Basic Sweeps:
Scissor Sweep: From closed guard.
Hip Bump Sweep: Timing and technique from guard.
Flower Sweep (Pendulum): Advanced sweep introduced at later grey levels.

Positional Transitions:

Moving from mount to side control and vice versa.
Guard recovery drills (shrimping from side control or mount to return to guard).
Basic standup transitions (technical standup, guard passing to standing).

5. Guard Passing (Developing Offense)

By the time students reach advanced grey levels, they should be comfortable passing various guards using both standing and kneeling passes.

Basic Guard Passing:
Standing Guard Break: Standing up to open a closed guard.
Knee Slice Pass: Cutting through the opponent's guard with control.
Stack Pass: Overcoming legs using pressure.

Intermediate Guard Passing:
Torreando (Bullfighter) Pass: Using angles to pass the guard.
XPass (Step Over): A dynamic, fast pass for open guard situations.

6. Defensive Skills (Developing a Solid Defense)

Building a solid defense is important for longevity and confidence in BJJ. Children should learn to defend themselves in all positions, focusing on safety and escaping bad positions.

Basic Defenses and Escapes:
Mount Escapes: Trapandroll (upa), shrimp escape.
Guard Retention: Defending passes using frames and hip movement.
Side Control Escapes: Using hip escapes, framing to recover guard.
Back Escape: Escaping hooks and turning into guard or turtle position.

7. Drills and Positional Sparring (Structured Training)

Structured drills and positional sparring help reinforce techniques in a safe environment. These sessions are a key part of the children's curriculum, designed to ensure practical application while keeping competition in check.

Positional Drills:
Mount escapes: Set a timer, and one child tries to escape while the other maintains control.
Guard retention drills: One partner tries to pass guard, while the other defends.
Sweeps vs. submissions: Guard player tries to sweep or submit while the top player defends.

Games to Reinforce Techniques:
Sharks & Minnows: Players in bottom mount must escape as quickly as possible. Winners move to the next round.
King of the Hill: Kids take turns trying to pass the guard of a "king" (one student), switching roles upon success.

8. Character Development and Values (Teaching Life Lessons through BJJ)

Brazilian Jiu Jitsu for children isn't just about physical skills. A huge part of the curriculum focuses on character development—instilling values like discipline, respect, perseverance, and teamwork.

Respect for Instructors and Peers: Bowing in and out of class, showing respect through etiquette.
Discipline: Understanding the importance of consistent training and effort.
Teamwork and Cooperation: Working with partners in drills, encouraging others.
Sportsmanship: Handling wins and losses gracefully, tapping early to avoid injury, and helping peers grow.

Overall Curriculum Progression

1. White Belt Entry Level:
   Focus: Basic positions (mount, guard, side control), basic movements, fundamental escapes, introduction to a few simple submissions (e.g., Americana, armbar).
   Emphasis: Safety, body awareness, and respect.

2. Grey Belt Foundational:
   Focus: Refinement of positions, introduction of open guard, simple sweeps, additional submissions (e.g., triangle, rear naked choke).
   Emphasis: Guard retention, smooth transitions, introduction to standing guard passes.

3. Grey Intermediate:
   Focus: More dynamic movement, expanded sweeps, advanced positional control (e.g., back control), advanced escapes (side control escapes to guard recovery), chaining submissions (e.g., armbar to triangle).
   Emphasis: Fluid transitions, maintaining offensive pressure, deeper understanding of defense.

4. Grey Advanced
   Focus: More complex passing (e.g., Torreando pass), greater control from dominant positions, submissions from multiple positions, positional dominance.
   Emphasis: Combining movements, timing, strategy, preparation for higherlevel belts.

Final Thoughts on White to Grey Belt Curriculum

The journey from white to grey belt for children is one of growth, both physically and mentally. The curriculum ensures that children build a strong technical foundation while developing the values central to BJJ. As they progress through the grey belt ranks, children become more proficient at transitioning between positions, applying submissions, and thinking strategically. By the end of their grey belt journey, they should have a solid grasp of BJJ's core principles and be ready to enter the more advanced colored belts (yellow, orange, green) with confidence.

For children progressing from grey to yellow belt in Brazilian Jiu Jitsu (BJJ), the focus intensifies on refining their techniques and introducing more advanced concepts while continuing to emphasize the core values of discipline, respect, and sportsmanship. The transition from grey to yellow is significant, as students move from foundational knowledge to a deeper, more strategic understanding of BJJ, preparing them for the challenges of higher belt levels.

This curriculum will cover all the variations of grey belts into yellow (greywhite, greyblack) and the single yellow belt, consolidating the development required across these stages.

Core Concepts from Grey to Yellow Belt (All Levels)

Technical Refinement: Continued development of previously learned techniques with more precise execution and a focus on the details of each position, submission, and escape.
Combinations and Transitions: Students should begin linking techniques together more fluidly—moving from sweeps to submissions, escapes to reversals, and guard retention to offensive attacks.
Strategy and Timing: Understanding the importance of timing, pressure, and momentum in both offense and defense.
Positional Control and Dominance: Greater emphasis on dominating positions (mount, side control, back control) and maintaining control under pressure.
Mental Growth: Building the resilience, patience, and humility needed to continue growing in BJJ and life.

Curriculum: Grey to Yellow Belt (All Grey Belt Variations to Yellow)

1. Advanced Movements and Body Mechanics

By this stage, children should be mastering body mechanics that allow them to move efficiently and dynamically. These movements will enhance their ability to control an opponent or escape difficult positions.

Advanced Shrimping Variations:
   Sidetoside shrimping drills combined with turtle and guard recovery.
   Shrimping under pressure (with a partner trying to pin them).

Granby Rolls: Learning how to use granby rolls to recover guard or transition to an advantageous position.

Turtle Position Recovery: Emphasizing mobility from turtle and returning to guard or transitioning to sweeps.

Technical StandUp Under Pressure: Practicing standup while a partner applies pressure to simulate real escape scenarios.

2. Positional Mastery and Transitions

As they progress from grey to yellow belt, students will be expected to have a deeper understanding of positional hierarchy, control, and transition. They should be comfortable with moving between positions and maintaining control in more advanced scenarios.

Mount:
  Top: Emphasizing transitioning between attacks (e.g., switching between Americana, armbar, and choke attempts).
  Bottom: More advanced escapes using combinations of bridging and shrimping. Introduction to reversing mount into more dominant positions like half guard or full guard.

Guard (Top and Bottom):
  Closed Guard: Continued refinement of attacks from closed guard (setting up sweeps and submissions in combination).
  Open Guard Concepts: Greater emphasis on using open guard to offbalance the opponent, including spider guard, lasso guard, and De La Riva.
  Sweeps: Refining sweeps like scissor sweep, hip bump sweep, and flower sweep, while introducing more complex sweeps like De La Riva sweep and butterfly sweep.

Side Control:
  Top: Advanced control drills, transitioning between side control and mount/kneeonbelly to maintain pressure.
  Bottom: More fluid escapes, combining hip escapes with guard recovery, framing, and transitioning to standing.

Back Control:
  Top: Refining back control, focusing on keeping hooks in while attacking with the rear naked choke or transitioning to armbars.
  Bottom: Learning advanced back escapes, including peeling hooks and turning into guard or turtle.

Turtle Position:
  Top: Controlling an opponent in turtle, transitioning to attacks like clock choke or rolling into back control.
  Bottom: Defensive strategies, recovering guard, or escaping to a better position.

3. Submissions and Submission Chains (Combinations)

Students at this level should be learning how to combine submission attempts into chains, ensuring that if one submission fails, they can transition smoothly to another.

Core Submissions (Refined):
  Americana (Keylock): From mount, side control, and even guard.

Armbar: Fluidity in transitioning from mount and guard.
Triangle Choke: Improved setup from guard, using momentum and angles.
Rear Naked Choke (RNC): Combining back control with transitions into the choke.

New Submissions Introduced:
  Kimura: From guard, top side control, and northsouth position.
  Omoplata: As a followup to a failed triangle or as a sweep from guard.
  Bow and Arrow Choke: From back control or turtle position.

Submission Chains:
  Armbar to Triangle: Learning to flow between armbar and triangle choke depending on the opponent's defense.
  Kimura to Armbar: Combining these two attacks for efficiency.
  Triangle to Omoplata: Flowing from one submission to another to keep the opponent off balance.

Submission Defense:
  Continued focus on escaping or defending armbar, triangle, and rear naked choke.
  Learning gripbreaking techniques to counter Kimura and Americana.

4. Advanced Sweeps and Guard Passing

This stage of development will see students refining their sweeping techniques and guard passes, learning how to execute them with more precision and fluidity.

Advanced Sweeps:
  Butterfly Sweep: Sweeping from open guard using hooks and momentum.
  De La Riva Sweep: Leveraging the opponent's base to offbalance them.
  XGuard Sweep: Introduction to Xguard concepts and basic sweeps.

Refining Guard Passes:
  Torreando (Bullfighter) Pass: More fluidity and timing.
  Leg Drag Pass: Learning how to drag the opponent's leg and pass into side control or mount.
  OverUnder Pass: Introducing a pressureheavy pass, transitioning to side control.

Dynamic Guard Passing: Combining guard passes into sequences. For example, moving from knee slice to leg drag if the opponent defends.

5. Defensive Strategy and Counterattacks

As children progress toward the yellow belt, their defensive skills should be more advanced, allowing them to not only escape but counterattack effectively.

Advanced Guard Retention:
  Combining frames, hip movement, and sweeps to defend guard passes.
  Learning how to regain guard from scrambles or after failed sweeps.

Positional Escapes (Refined):
  More fluid mount escapes (upas combined with shrimping).
  Side control escapes with the addition of frames and explosive hip movements.
  Defending kneeonbelly transitions and learning to counter with sweeps or guard recovery.

Counterattacks from Defense:
  Attacking submissions during an opponent's guard pass attempt (e.g., armbar or triangle setup while they pass guard).
  Sweeping during submission attempts (e.g., transitioning from a failed armbar to a sweep from guard).

6. Sparring and Drills (Positional and Full Sparring)

Sparring is crucial at this stage, with more emphasis on controlled, thoughtful sparring rather than aggressive competition. Children will engage in positional sparring, focusing on specific techniques, and eventually moving into full sparring.

Positional Sparring Focus:
  Mount: Maintaining mount vs. escaping to guard.
  Guard: Retention and passing drills (one child tries to pass guard while the other defends or sweeps).
  Side Control: Maintaining top pressure vs. bottom escapes and guard recovery.
  Back Control: Attacking submissions from back control vs. escapes and transitioning to guard.

Full Sparring (Introduction):
  Controlled rolling with partners, emphasizing technique over strength.
  Encouraging strategic thinking during sparring—flowing between offense and defense.

Timed Sparring Rounds: Short rounds to focus on endurance, technique retention under pressure, and mental focus.

7. Character Development and Values (Mental Growth)

As students progress to yellow belt, the emphasis on character development continues, reinforcing values learned in earlier belts while encouraging higher levels of discipline and responsibility.

Discipline and Focus: Commitment to regular training and selfimprovement.
Resilience and Patience: Learning to deal with losses, frustration, and the longterm journey of BJJ.
Respect and Sportsmanship: Continued emphasis on respect for training partners, coaches, and opponents in competition or sparring.
Leadership: Beginning to take on leadership roles in the class (helping younger or less experienced students).

Overall Curriculum Progression (Grey to Yellow Belt)

1. GreyWhite Belt:
   Focus: Refining basic sweeps, submissions, and positional transitions. Learning the first few submission chains and focusing on guard retention.
   Emphasis: Fluidity between positions, developing a basic strategic mindset.

2. Grey Belt:
   Focus: Introduction of more complex submissions, like omoplata and bow and arrow choke. Continued guard passing and sweeps with more dynamic entries.
   Emphasis: Strategy and timing, understanding how to blend offense with defense.

3. GreyBlack Belt:
   Focus: Mastery of existing submissions and sweeps, adding advanced submissions like Kimura and submission chains.
   Emphasis: Positional dominance, advanced escapes, and developing strategic sparring skills.

4. Yellow Belt:
   Focus: Consolidating all learned techniques, mastering transitions between submissions, sweeps, and positions. Emphasis on leadership in class and a deeper understanding of the art.
   Emphasis: Becoming a more well rounded practitioner with the ability to think strategically in both competition and class settings.

Final Thoughts on Grey to Yellow Belt Curriculum

The progression from grey to yellow belt marks a key developmental stage where children shift from fundamental skills to a more advanced understanding of Brazilian Jiu Jitsu. By the time students reach yellow belt, they should have a solid technical base, the ability to transition between moves fluidly, and the mental resilience to continue their BJJ journey. Additionally, the values instilled through the discipline of training will prepare them not just for future belts but for challenges in life.

The transition from yellow belt to orange belt in youth Brazilian Jiu Jitsu (BJJ) is a crucial stage, as it represents a deeper shift in technical ability, strategic thinking, and personal growth. This stage of development will see the student expand upon their already solid foundation, refine their technique, and incorporate more complex strategies into their game. Additionally, the student will begin to gain a more profound understanding of timing, leverage, and control, while also learning to manage physical and mental challenges with increased resilience.

The following curriculum is designed to encompass all the variations within the yellow belt range, from yellowwhite to yellowblack belt, ultimately leading to the orange belt.

Core Concepts for Yellow to Orange Belt (All Yellow Belt Variations)

Refining Advanced Techniques: Students should not only understand the technique but be able to execute it smoothly under pressure and against stronger or more skilled opponents.
Positional Control & Pressure: Emphasizing heavier, more deliberate control from top positions, and recognizing the importance of constant pressure.
Strategic Awareness: Introducing concepts of offensive and defensive strategy in different positions, especially guard, mount, and back control.
Timing and Reaction: Students should develop the ability to react faster, anticipate their opponent's moves, and exploit openings effectively.
Mental and Emotional Growth: Preparing for the emotional challenges of competition and the higher expectations placed on them as they rise in rank.

Curriculum: Yellow to Orange Belt (All Yellow Belt Variations to Orange)

1. Body Movement and Advanced Drills

As they progress, students will need to further enhance their understanding of body mechanics and develop the ability to move with greater efficiency, agility, and control. The drills here should prepare them for more dynamic rolling situations and competitionlevel sparring.

Rolling Drills (Continuous Movement):
  Drill that incorporates various transitions (from mount to back, from side control to guard, etc.) without stopping.
  Emphasizing positional control and keeping pressure during transitions.

Rolling SidetoSide Guard Retention:
  Learning how to recover guard by moving side to side, incorporating legs and hips to block passes.

Granby Roll into Submission/Guard Recovery:
  Using the Granby roll not only to recover guard but also to set up submissions (e.g., transitioning into an armbar or triangle).

Dynamic StandUp Drills:
  Using technical standups while an opponent is trying to close distance, allowing them to practice maintaining space or transitioning into takedown defense.

2. Advanced Positional Understanding and Transitions

At this level, students will need to focus on gaining a deeper understanding of positional hierarchy and how to control an opponent more effectively. They must demonstrate greater efficiency in both offensive and defensive positional control.

Mount:

Top Mount: Focus on isolating limbs for submission attacks (such as setting up mounted triangles or transitioning from armbar to choke).
Bottom Mount: Advanced escapes like rolling into single leg Xguard or recovering into deep halfguard.

Side Control:
Top Side Control: Introduce "killing the hips," using advanced positional pressure to stop the opponent from shrimping or recovering guard.
Bottom Side Control: Introducing the use of frames and elbowknee escapes to create space for advanced recoveries.

Guard (Top and Bottom):
Open Guard: Refining De La Riva guard, incorporating sweeps, and transitioning to Xguard.
Spider Guard: Developing a stronger spider guard game, learning to maintain grips and offbalance the opponent.
Closed Guard: Advanced techniques like trapping arms for cross collar chokes, overhook to triangle setups, and sweeptosubmission transitions.

Back Control:
Top: Developing the ability to transition smoothly from back control to mounted triangle or bow and arrow choke.
Bottom: Refining back escapes under heavy pressure, learning to counter choke attempts with sweeps or reversals.

Turtle:
Top Turtle: Continued development of clock choke and crucifix setups, maintaining tight control and the ability to transition to back control.
Bottom Turtle: More advanced guard recovery and escapes using momentum and counters, introducing the granby roll to regain guard or transition.

3. Submissions and Submission Chains

Submissions at this stage should become more dynamic and include a greater focus on chaining techniques together. Students should learn to capitalize on submission opportunities by transitioning seamlessly between them, as well as how to apply them under stress.

Core Submissions (Refined):
Armbar Variations: From mount, guard, and side control, with a focus on maintaining control even if the initial attempt is countered.
Triangle: Refining setups from both guard and mount, learning to finish the triangle in various positions (such as transitioning to an armbar if the triangle fails).
Kimura and Americana: Setting up the Kimura from standing and guard, and understanding how to combine these attacks into sweep opportunities.

New Submissions Introduced:
Ezekiel Choke: Learning how to apply this choke effectively from mount and back control.

Guillotine (Basic & ArmIn): From standing and closed guard, learning how to apply guillotine as a defense against takedown attempts or during scrambles.

Triangle Armbar Combination: Transitioning from a triangle setup into an armbar and vice versa, increasing submission flow.

Clock Choke: Refining the application of the clock choke from turtle, adding pressure and timing.

Submission Chains:

Armbar to Triangle to Omoplata: Developing a smooth transition chain between these techniques from closed guard.

Kimura to Sweep or Armbar: Understanding how to transition from a Kimura attempt to either sweep the opponent or switch to an armbar.

Rear Naked Choke to Bow and Arrow: Combining two submissions from back control, giving the student options depending on the opponent's defense.

Submission Defense:

Improved defense against common submissions like armbars, triangles, guillotines, and leg locks.

Recognizing the setups for more advanced submissions and learning how to shut them down before they fully develop.

4. Advanced Guard Passing and Sweeps

Guard passing and sweeps should become more technical and fluid, with a greater emphasis on recognizing when to transition between passes or sweeps to exploit the opponent's mistakes.

Advanced Guard Passing:

Leg Drag Pass: Refining the leg drag pass with greater control and transitioning immediately into dominant side control or mount.

Knee Slice Pass: Emphasizing pressure and controlling the opponent's hips to finish the pass effectively.

OverUnder Pass: Developing greater fluidity in passing from closed guard into side control or mount.

Torreando Pass to Mount: Transitioning from this speed pass directly into a dominant mount position.

Advanced Sweeps:

XGuard Sweeps: Introduction to Xguard sweeps and transitioning into back control or leg attacks.

Butterfly Guard Sweeps: Refining butterfly guard techniques, focusing on offbalancing a larger opponent and transitioning into dominant positions.

De La Riva Sweeps to Back Take: Using De La Riva guard sweeps to transition directly into taking the back.

5. Defensive Tactics and Counterattacks

A key aspect of moving from yellow to orange is developing a solid defensive game. Students must understand not only how to defend themselves from bad positions or submissions but also how to counterattack effectively from defense.

Guard Retention (Refined):
Defending guard passes with better timing and control, incorporating inversion (rolling to defend passes) and using lasso guard to maintain control.

Advanced Positional Escapes:
Mount Escapes: More dynamic mount escapes, focusing on using the bridge and roll technique while combining it with legtrap transitions.
Side Control Escapes: Creating space and framing for better guard recovery or transitioning into single leg Xguard from side control.
Turtle Escapes: Using granby rolls and guard recovery to escape from the turtle position under heavy pressure.

Counterattacks from Defense:
Attacking directly after escaping positions like side control or mount (e.g., sweeping from half guard after a failed mount escape).
Submissions from bottom positions when the opponent attempts to pass (e.g., armbar or triangle attempts during the opponent's guard pass).

6. Sparring and Drills (Positional and Full Sparring)

Sparring becomes more integral to the student's growth at this stage. There should be a focus on maintaining composure and executing techniques under pressure.

Positional Sparring Focus:
Mount: Top students work on isolating arms and finishing submissions, while bottom students work on recovering guard or escaping.
Guard: Practicing sweeps, submissions, and passes in controlled rounds of positional sparring (focus on flow and timing).
Back Control: Top students aim to control and submit, while bottom students focus on escapes and reversing positions.

Full Sparring (Increased Intensity):
Introducing longer rounds to test endurance, patience, and strategy.
Allowing students to spar with greater intensity, encouraging them to implement strategy rather than relying on strength or speed.

Situational Sparring: Short rounds where students are placed in challenging positions (e.g., stuck in mount, defending a choke, etc.) and must escape or defend before time runs out.

7. Mental and Emotional Resilience Development

At the yellow belt level, emphasis on mental and emotional resilience is crucial. Students must learn how to handle adversity on and off the mat.

Goal Setting: Encouraging students to set short and longterm goals, both in their BJJ journey and personal life.
Resilience Training: Techniques for managing stress during competition and the importance of learning from losses.
Leadership Skills: Opportunities for students to lead drills and assist in teaching newer students, fostering a sense of responsibility and mentorship.

Final Thoughts on Yellow to Orange Belt Curriculum

The transition from yellow belt to orange belt serves as a crucial period of development for young BJJ practitioners. The focus on advanced techniques, strategic thinking, and mental resilience will help shape them not only as martial artists but as individuals prepared to face challenges both inside and outside the dojo. By fostering a love for the art and instilling valuable life skills, this curriculum aims to prepare students for continued success in their BJJ journey.

Here's a comprehensive curriculum for the transition from orange belt to green belt in youth Brazilian Jiu Jitsu (BJJ). This stage builds upon the foundational techniques and concepts learned at the orange belt level, allowing students to refine their skills, develop greater strategic thinking, and enhance their mental and emotional resilience.

Core Concepts for Orange to Green Belt

Technical Mastery: Deepening understanding of techniques and improving execution under pressure.
Strategic Depth: Introducing more complex strategies, counterstrategies, and situational awareness during rolling.
Physical and Mental Conditioning: Enhancing physical attributes while fostering mental resilience and composure in competitive scenarios.
Leadership and Mentorship: Encouraging students to take on more leadership roles in class and support their peers.

Curriculum: Orange to Green Belt (All Orange Belt Variations to Green)

1. Advanced Movement and Drills

At this level, students should focus on advanced body mechanics, fluidity of movement, and application of techniques in dynamic scenarios.

Dynamic Flow Drills:
  Partner drills focusing on transitioning between positions and submissions fluidly, emphasizing continuity of motion.
  Creating sequences that connect techniques (e.g., sweeps leading into submissions).

Specific Guard Recovery Drills:
  Partnered drills that emphasize recovering guard against a resisting opponent.
  Working on leg entanglements and quick recoveries to standing.

Shadow Rolling:
  Practicing movements and techniques without a partner to build muscle memory and improve fluidity.

2. Positional Control and Advanced Techniques

A strong focus on positional control, efficiency, and execution of techniques in various positions is essential. This section enhances the ability to hold and escape from dominant positions effectively.

Mount Control:
  Top Mount: Mastering the ability to maintain and transition from mount to back control or submissions (e.g., bow and arrow choke, armbar).
  Bottom Mount: Advanced escapes, including hip escapes and using momentum to create space.

Side Control:
  Top Side Control: Learning to apply pressure while maintaining control, using transitions to kneeonbelly and back.
  Bottom Side Control: Emphasizing escapes to half guard and open guard with a focus on frames.

Back Control:
  Top: Mastering the mechanics of back control, focusing on maintaining hooks, controlling the opponent's hips, and developing choke setups (e.g., RNC, sliding collar choke).
  Bottom: Understanding how to escape from back control and transition into guard recovery.

Guard Mechanics:
  Closed Guard: Advanced submissions (e.g., crosscollar chokes, pendulum sweeps) and transitions to open guard.
  Open Guard: Using various grips (De La Riva, spider, lasso) to set up sweeps and submissions effectively.

3. Submissions and Counter Submission Techniques

Refinement of submission techniques and developing an understanding of countering submissions will be emphasized in this section.

Refined Submission Techniques:
  Armbar Variations: Focusing on setups from multiple positions, including mounted and open guard variations.

Triangle Chokes: Mastering setups from closed guard and understanding how to combine triangle attempts with armbars or sweeps.
Kimura Variations: Learning to transition from the kimura to other submissions or sweeps.

New Submissions:
Anaconda Choke: Learning setups from side control and half guard.
Omoplata: Focusing on entries and setups from guard, including how to transition to sweeps or back takes.

Submission Counter Techniques:
Understanding common defense against armbars, triangles, and chokes, with drills focusing on countering attempts effectively.
Transitioning from submission defense to sweeps or counterattacks.

4. Guard Passing Techniques and Strategies

This section aims to refine guard passing techniques and develop strategic approaches to breaking guards.

Advanced Guard Passing:
Leg Drag: Emphasizing control of the opponent's hips and legs while executing the pass effectively.
Knee Slice: Mastering the knee slice pass to maintain pressure and transition into dominant positions.
OverUnder Pass: Building fluidity in executing the overunder pass, with attention to balance and body mechanics.

Guard Passing Drills:
Partner drills focusing on passing different types of guard (closed, open, half) while under resistance.
Situational sparring where one partner plays guard while the other works on passing techniques.

Counter Guard Passing Techniques:
Understanding how to defend against guard passes with escapes and sweeps.
Developing quick recovery techniques from failed pass attempts.

5. Sparring and Competition Preparation

Sparring is crucial at this stage to test techniques and strategies under pressure. The focus should be on applying learned skills in realistic scenarios.

Positional Sparring:
Structured rounds focusing on specific positions (mount, side control, guard), allowing students to practice techniques against resistance.

Situational Sparring:
  Focusing on specific scenarios, such as escaping mount, defending submissions, or passing guard.

Full Sparring:
  Longer rounds with an emphasis on applying learned techniques in a freerolling format.
  Encouraging students to experiment with strategies and tactics during rolling sessions.

6. Leadership Development and Mentorship

As students progress, it's important to foster leadership skills and encourage mentorship within the class.

Mentorship Opportunities:
  Assigning students to help newer practitioners, fostering a sense of responsibility and community.

Teaching Techniques:
  Students should be encouraged to lead warmup drills or demonstrate techniques to peers, enhancing their understanding and confidence.

Team Building Activities:
  Engaging in drills or activities that promote teamwork, communication, and mutual support among students.

7. Mental and Emotional Resilience Training

Building resilience is essential for young practitioners to handle competition and adversity both on and off the mat.

Mindfulness Techniques:
  Teaching students mindfulness and visualization techniques to enhance focus and reduce anxiety in competitive situations.

Goal Setting and Reflection:
  Encouraging students to set personal goals for their training and performance while reflecting on their progress.

Dealing with Loss and Setbacks:
  Discussing the importance of learning from losses and the value of perseverance in the face of challenges.

Final Thoughts on Orange to Green Belt Curriculum

The transition from orange belt to green belt marks a significant phase of growth in youth BJJ practitioners. The emphasis on technical mastery, strategic thinking, and emotional resilience will prepare students not only for their journey in martial arts but also for challenges in their everyday lives. By fostering a supportive and empowering training environment, this curriculum aims to instill a love for BJJ while cultivating valuable life skills that extend beyond the mat.

Glossary of Terms and Concepts

This glossary provides brief definitions and explanations for easy reference.

Positions:

Mount: A dominant position where one person is sitting on top of the opponent's torso. The person on top has control and leverage, while the bottom person is at a disadvantage.

Side Control (Side Mount): A position where the person on top is lying across the opponent's body, controlling their upper body and hips. The top person can transition to other positions or set up submissions.

Back Control: The most dominant position, where the person on top is behind the opponent, controlling them with hooks (legs wrapped around the body) and grips, typically seeking a rear naked choke.

Guard: A position where the person on the bottom uses their legs to control or defend against the person on top. There are various types of guard positions (closed guard, open guard, butterfly guard, etc.).

Closed Guard: A type of guard where the bottom person's legs are wrapped around the opponent's waist, maintaining control and defending against passes while looking for sweeps or submissions.

Open Guard: A variation of guard where the legs are not locked around the opponent. Open guard includes several subtypes such as spider guard, butterfly guard, and De La Riva guard.

Half Guard: A guard position where the bottom person has one of the top person's legs trapped between their own legs. The goal is typically to sweep or regain full guard.

Turtle: A defensive position where the person on bottom curls up on their hands and knees, protecting themselves from attacks but vulnerable to being rolled or having their back taken.

KneeonBelly: A dominant top position where the attacker places one knee on the opponent's abdomen, applying pressure while transitioning to other positions or submissions.

Submissions:

Armbar: A submission that targets the elbow joint by hyperextending the arm. It can be applied from multiple positions, including mount, guard, and side control.

Triangle Choke: A submission where the legs are wrapped around the opponent's neck and arm, cutting off blood flow to the brain by compressing the carotid arteries. Often applied from guard.

Rear Naked Choke (RNC): A choke applied from back control where the attacker encircles the opponent's neck with the arms, cutting off blood flow to the brain.

Americana (Keylock): A shoulder lock where the opponent's arm is bent at a 90degree angle and twisted to apply pressure on the shoulder joint. Commonly executed from mount or side control.

Kimura: A shoulder lock that twists the arm behind the opponent's back, creating pressure on the shoulder joint. It can be applied from guard, side control, or even standing positions.

Guillotine Choke: A front headlock submission where the opponent's neck is trapped and compressed against the attacker's arm, often applied when the opponent attempts a takedown.

Bow and Arrow Choke: A gi choke applied from back control where the attacker grips the opponent's collar and uses their legs to stretch the opponent, mimicking the motion of drawing a bow.

Ezekiel Choke: A choke often performed from mount or back control where the attacker uses their own sleeve or gi to apply pressure to the opponent's neck.

Omoplata: A shoulder lock applied from guard by isolating the opponent's arm with the legs and rotating the body to apply pressure to the shoulder joint.

Anaconda Choke: A submission where the attacker threads their arm under the opponent's neck and opposite arm, then rolls to apply pressure to choke the opponent.

Sweeps:

Scissor Sweep: A sweep from closed guard where the attacker uses their legs in a scissor motion to offbalance the opponent and take them to the ground.

Hip Bump Sweep: A simple sweep from guard where the attacker bumps their hips into the opponent's torso, knocking them over and reversing the position.

Pendulum Sweep (Flower Sweep): A sweep from guard where the attacker uses a swinging leg motion to generate momentum and sweep the opponent to the side.

Butterfly Sweep: A sweep executed from butterfly guard by using hooks with the legs to elevate the opponent and transition into a dominant position.

De La Riva Sweep: A sweep from De La Riva guard (with one leg hooking the opponent's outside thigh) that uses leverage and momentum to offbalance and sweep the opponent.

XGuard Sweep: A sweep from Xguard (where the attacker's legs entangle one of the opponent's legs) that allows the attacker to sweep or transition to a standing position.

Guard Passing:

Knee Slice Pass: A guard pass where the attacker drives their knee through the opponent's legs while controlling their upper body, transitioning to side control.

Torreando (Bullfighter) Pass: A standing pass where the attacker grabs the opponent's pants and pulls the legs to the side while moving around them, like a matador avoiding a bull.

Leg Drag Pass: A guard pass where the attacker pins the opponent's leg across their body and uses it to pass to side control or back control.

Stack Pass: A pass from closed guard where the attacker stacks the opponent by driving their knees toward their face, opening the guard and passing to side control.

OverUnder Pass: A guard pass where the attacker drives under one leg of the opponent while controlling the other, using pressure to flatten the opponent and pass the guard.

Escapes and Defensive Movements:

Shrimping (Hip Escape): A fundamental movement where the practitioner moves their hips away from the opponent to create space, commonly used to escape mount or side control.

Bridging: A movement where the practitioner arches their hips to disrupt the opponent's base, commonly used to escape from mount or side control.

Technical StandUp: A movement that allows the practitioner to stand up safely while maintaining a defensive posture, often used when escaping from bottom positions.

Granby Roll: A rolling movement used to escape positions like side control or turtle, where the practitioner rolls over their shoulders to regain guard or escape a bad position.

Elbow Escape: A specific escape from mount or side control where the practitioner uses their elbow to create space and recover guard or half guard.

Advanced Guard Systems:

Spider Guard: An open guard where the attacker uses grips on the opponent's sleeves and places their feet on the opponent's biceps to control posture and set up sweeps or submissions.

De La Riva Guard: An open guard where one leg hooks the opponent's outside thigh, and the attacker controls the opponent's posture, often leading to sweeps or back takes.

Butterfly Guard: A seated open guard where the attacker uses hooks with their feet on the inside of the opponent's thighs, often used to sweep or transition into submissions.

XGuard: A guard position where the attacker's legs are entangled around one of the opponent's legs, creating leverage for sweeps and attacks.

Lasso Guard: A variation of open guard where one leg is wrapped around the opponent's arm, using the gi sleeve grip to control the opponent and set up sweeps or submissions.

Miscellaneous Terms and Concepts:

Positional Hierarchy: The system of ranking positions in BJJ from most dominant to least dominant. Generally, back control is considered the most dominant, followed by mount, side control, and guard.

Hooks: Refers to using the feet or legs to control the opponent, especially in positions like back control or butterfly guard.

Frames: Using the arms or elbows to create space and defend against pressure, especially when trying to escape positions like mount or side control.

Base: The ability to maintain balance and prevent being swept or destabilized by an opponent.

Submission Chains: Linking multiple submission attempts together so that if one fails, another is immediately available (e.g., transitioning from an armbar to a triangle choke).

Flow Rolling: Light, continuous rolling focused on movement and transitions without intense resistance, often used for practice or as a warmup.

Mindset and Philosophy:

Composure Under Pressure: The ability to stay calm and focused while in difficult or disadvantageous positions, a key component of BJJ's mental game.

Growth Mindset: Emphasizing continuous improvement, learning from mistakes, and being open to new techniques and strategies.

Leadership and Mentorship: As students progress to higher belts, they are expected to take on more of a mentorship role, helping guide lower belts and contributing to the overall learning environment.

Humility: Recognizing that BJJ is a lifelong journey where progress is often slow and that there is always more to learn, no matter one's rank or skill level.

Notes: We recommend you start a journal to log your lessons at the beginning and refer back to them before class to help you get back to where you left off from your last class. Here are 15 pages for you to begin.